E-Therapy Lectures

What Integration is About
The Four Unthinkables
The Easiest Way

A. L. Kitselman

Published in the USA and the UK
by

MASTERWORKS INTERNATIONAL
27 Old Gloucester Street
London
WC1N 3XX
UK

Email: admin@mwipublishing.com
Web: http:/www.mwipublishing.com

ISBN: 978-0-9565803-8-2
copyright © A. L. Kitselman 1960, 2013

Cover by mywizarddesign.com © Morag Campbell

Contents

Publisher's Preface

The Institute of Integration founded by A. L. Kitselman was one of the largest publishers of taped lectures on the topic of personal psychological integration in the 1950s. This book is composed of three small booklets that were themselves transcriptions of extemporaneous taped recorded lectures given by A.L. Kitselman between 1952 - 1954.

The three books that comprise this volume are "What Integration is About" from a talk given on November 12th 1952. "The Four Unthinkables", a talk given on June 7th 1954 and "The Easiest Way" (Group E and Hyper E) a talk given on November 12th 1952.

FOREWARD

My father, first and foremost, was a student and a teacher.

He studied many different philosophies, religions and people throughout his life. He took all the knowledge he could find on the power of the inner self and taught people how to better themselves using their own inner power.

As a child I was taught these things not knowing I was being schooled, as they were the way things were done in our house. "We need to become aware of the big picture," one of his favorite sayings, and it will help in relieving any pain.

He did not see the bad side of people. He also use to say, "I would rather believe in people and be wrong, than to not believe and be right," that has always been my favorite.

We had many visitors who came for E-sessions; they were just a part of our daily lives. Many came back time after time and became family friends. Later they were part of the Institute of Integration. Some even became teachers of E-Therapy and helped others.

Our house was always full of interesting people; we even had Buddhists monks stay with us. It all seemed normal at the time. You never knew who would be at the house when you returned from school, but you knew they would end up your friend.

His teaching, "To realize a state of being in which there is no obstruction."

He was a great father to me and a teacher to many.

I hope his work will enlighten your path in life.

Khema Rani Kitselman (Siemers)

What Integration is About

Many people seem to understand the general idea of healing—you have migraine headaches, you go through some process of healing and then you don't have migraine headaches any more—but there are quite a few who do not really understand what <u>integration</u> is. If I suffer from migraine, and then, after a while, I no longer suffer from migraine, it is easy to see in what direction I have moved. But if I am not now integrated, and I then achieve the first degree of integration, or the second degree of integration, in what direction have I moved? What kind of changes have been made in me? I should like to discuss three fields, and these three fields might be described as the field of sensuality, the field of esthetics, and the field of fulfilment, or attainment. These are three fields in which one moves if one takes up the work of personal integration.

Sensuality—what does that mean? It means desire for pleasure through the physical—one can have a sensual <u>craving</u>. 'Sensual' is ordinarily used to mean 'sexual', but it has other meanings. One can have a sensual craving for a steak, or to own a fine piece of brocade fabric. You might say that physical possession, physical indulgence, is what comes under the heading of 'sensual'.

Now, in reference to sensual things, it is necessary to know and understand what is attractive about them, what is repellent about them, and how to get beyond them. So far as sensual pleasures are concerned, we see things with the eye, we hear sounds with the ear, we detect odors with the nose, we perceive flavors with the tongue, and we can feel touch upon the body. Some of the things which we can perceive in these five ways are desirable, agreeable, pleasant and attractive, pleasurable and exciting to passion. That is, we get excited about them, we cling to them, we get bound up with them. We all know how that is so, with various physical possessions. To possess certain foods, certain furnishings, certain homes, certain clothing, certain physical possessions—these impulses come under the heading of sensuality, and it is undeniably true that in reference to things perceived through the eye, the ear, the nose, the tongue, and the sense of touch (which is all over the body), that many of such experiences are indeed pleasurable, in some cases to a very high degree. That is, of course, what is attractive about sensuality.

What is it that is repellent about sensuality? Well, if we put our faith, put our interest, in physical possessions, we have to acquire them, we have to get busy to earn them, we have to devote ourselves to accumulating physical possessions, accumulating material wealth, whether this material wealth be in the form of a man or a woman, or in the form of any one of various objects. One of the difficulties is that all such material accumulations are insecure, and there is therefore insecurity that goes along with them. Insecurity is not pleasant. If one is not successful in achieving sufficient material wealth, one experiences misery as a result of that— that is, if one is devoted to the pursuit of material pleasures. If one is successful, then one has to worry about watching and guarding the physical possessions that one has. So material pleasures, while they undeniably have qualities which attract, also have a number of qualities that are repellent; there are a number of difficulties about them.

It might be interesting, therefore, to find out if there is any way to get along satisfactorily without being preoccupied with material things, and it seems that it is possible. Many of us feel that if we do not go after material pleasures, we automatically lead a life of material misery, but that is not necessarily true. It seems that there are some people in this world who are not concerned at all about material pleasures; they have so altered their constitution, their internal make-up, that they have no need of man or woman, sexually, they have no need for elegance in food, shelter, or clothing. Yet such people do not necessarily live like beggars; it is not necessary at all. Such people, simply because they need less, perhaps, than most of us do, live in reasonable comfort. But the point is, they do not give much thought to it; as Whitman put it, they "think not so brain-sickly of things". These people think not 'brain-sickly' about material matters, and, as a result, they may have a much better perspective in handling their material possessions than other people do. People who are too excited about material possessions can make great mistakes about them, their acquisitive impulse may run riot, and they may be 'sheared like lambs', so to speak, as a result of it. They may become over-optimistic in buying something, or acquiring something. The person who is not overly concerned about material pleasures has a far better perspective, is far more impartial, and is very likely to manage his affairs in the field of material values much better. I don't know whether you have noticed it or not, but you may go to any city, and you will find in that city a number of men who engage in lending money on houses. These men may own a large number of houses, or they may have mortgages on a large number of houses; they really have quite a lot of money, are quite wealthy, and yet, if you study them carefully, you will discover that they themselves do not engage very much in the pursuit of material pleasures—that is, they themselves live much more simply than most of us would if we had that amount of money. As a result of not being too preoccupied with the problem of material possessions, these men have a good sense of judgment, a good perspective that enables them to accumulate considerable wealth. So, realizing that it is possible to live so transformed that one is not so much preoccupied with material pleasures, and realizing that that mode of life actually may help in the direction of what material concerns one has—it is apparent that this is a field in which we can consider the question of integration.

The great majority of the human race are motivated toward the accumulation of material pleasures, motivated toward the sensual. And remember just what it costs, if one is so motivated. The impulse of acquisitiveness, which most of us have in us, that impulse of acquisitiveness which is allowed to run rampant under the name of ambition, and that factor of sensuality, that pursuit of sensual happiness which is very dominant in the world today, has been pointed out by one of the teachers of integration as causing a very large percentage of the world's trouble, and most of the people in the world are engaged in pursuing this goal of material happiness.

If someone comes and hands you a large sum of money, you may think that it would be very easy to go out and get so much material happiness. If you get your happiness out of a can of beer, it is very easy to see how you get that happiness. In other words, the material pleasure, the material happiness, seems so simple, so obvious, so inescapable, that we all run after it and yet, if you stop to think about the disadvantages, they are many. The question of insecurity is always involved, and the fact that, if one runs after material happiness, after gain and profit, there just doesn't happen to be enough for everyone, and automatically one gets into conflict, and into many of the troubles that come from conflict. Do you realize that perhaps 99% of all the crime in the world is due to the presence in the world's population of a great many people who are seeking material happiness, and do you realize that virtually all of the warfare or large-scale crime in the world is due to that same sort of thing, the seeking of material happiness?

Apparently, it is quite possible for people to live happily, in reasonable material circumstances, without being primarily motivated toward material happiness. So, in this first field, the field of sensuality, material happiness, we should understand that it has its advantages, it has its disadvantages, and that it is quite possible to get along without being pre-occupied with it, and in this there is an escape from sensuality; there is something higher, there is some-thing beyond it. In the field of integration, we are concerned with arriving at what is beyond it—learning how to get there, in one degree or another. So much for the field of sensuality, of material happiness.

In discussing material happiness, I mentioned that one may possess a man or a woman, and I am speaking there in the sense that the sexual possession of a particular person is much like possessing an object in one respect, and that is the material aspect. But there is another aspect, which I have already referred to as esthetic, the esthetic field. Thus, a man may use and possess a woman, for his physical pleasure— that is one thing, but on the other hand there is another aspect of his relationship with that woman which may or may not be connected with physical pleasure. He may idealize her, his mind may be in love with her appearance, her beauty, what she appears to be. It doesn't have to be a woman—his mind may be in love with symphonic music or pursuing the ideal of being an artist, or something of that sort. This esthetic preoccupation is a seeking of beauty, a pre-occupation with beauty; and just as one cannot deny that, for a man, the possession of a woman may be a physical pleasure, there is also his being enchanted by a woman, or a woman being enchanted by a man, which is a mental pleasure. In other words, we may be concerned with the appearance of a person and feel pleasure on seeing that person and thus experience a form of mental or esthetic happiness. Of course, it not only applies to persons; it may apply to arts, music, and so on. These things are mental pursuits—and again, we should know what are their advantages, what are their disadvantages, and if it is possible to get along without them.

I have already mentioned some of the advantages. It is an undeniable fact that some people, men or women, possess such beauty that they captivate the heart or the mind. It is an undeniable fact that this is so. Great happiness and pleasure come from this. The same is true of certain esthetic pursuits, art, science, literature, drama, etc. There is an enchantment that arises from these various pursuits.

What are the disadvantages? An obvious one, to begin at the beginning—if a man falls in love with a woman's beauty and he endeavors to possess it, mentally or physically or both, he will discover after a time that woman's beauty is a changing thing. It fades. If a woman falls in love with a man's beauty, she will discover that that beauty fades. It may fade very slowly over a long period of years; nevertheless, it fades, and the sum total effect on the individual is a disappointment. (I'm not speaking of a transcendental relationship; I'm talking about beauty itself—its own limitations.) In other words, if a man idealizes some woman, that woman, the beauty that he thus idealizes, may change— all sorts of things can happen to her. She may become sick or ill, or she may die, and something beautiful has been destroyed. She may become the possession of another man; that's a very effective knife in one's vitals. We read about it, we see it in motion pictures; it happens. That's another example of the destruction of an idealistic attachment. All kinds of horrible things may happen—things that are perhaps horrible because they are more quiet, such as aging, fading, moral sickness, or even just separation. In other words, being esthetically preoccupied with a man or a woman is very risky; in the long run it always winds up with loss. That is one of the disadvantages of being esthetically preoccupied.

Let us take the case of some particular profession, a profession of art or science. As I have mentioned in other lectures, I learned to do creative work of the first rank (I think) in the field of mathematics; that was an esthetic preoccupation. Mathematics intrigues me, and yet today I find that it intrigues me less than it did ten years ago. I have also found that there are certain operations in mathematics that I could do a few years back, which I can not do now. My grasp of the subject has faded away in much the same way that a man's idealized appreciation of a woman might. In other words, you might say that I was in love with the muse of mathematics, and yet I find that the muse of mathematics is aging and failing, or that my response to the muse of mathematics is aging and failing, so that that particular preoccupation has its disadvantages.

Is it possible to live quite happily without that? There seem to be some people who in some strange way are able to live without being preoccupied with either material happiness or this esthetic happiness. That does not mean that these people are esthetically insensitive -— not at all; they actually may be far more creative than those who are much more excited about esthetic values. I think you will find that some of the very greatest creators in the fields of the arts, men like Bach, Sibelius and da Vinci, were extraordinarily impartial, were not captivated, not enchanted by esthetic values, were able to use them with detachment, not bound up in them, not upset about them, not infatuated with them. So there have been people, and I think that in general they are among our more able people in the history of the world, who are not bound up with preoccupations such as esthetic perfection in human beings, in an art, or a profession.

That leaves us with the third field. This third field has to do with fulfilment, or attainment. I refer to those attainments of emotional intensity, which so many mystics have been excited about. They are described in the E—book as the experiences of <u>fire</u>, and they are very wonderful things. Let me tell just a little about them.

First, I am going to tell how we approach them. Suppose that you are lying on your own bed, barefoot, with your head up on a pillow, and you look down towards your feet.

You look at your foot, and perhaps you are mentally absorbed in contemplating the shape of the human foot. At such a time you are aware of your own body and you are looking at part of your own body; there is an element of objectivity here. That is, you are not desiring anything particular at that time; you are just looking in wonder at the shape of the human foot. That is one of the conditions of fire, one of the lesser ones. You have gotten a little bit away from the ordinary pulling and hauling of emotions and compulsions and desires; you are just looking at something objectively.

Again, suppose you are looking through a micro-scope, looking at some microbes, and you observe their shapes and different colors. You are looking at something quite different from your own body; you may not be conscious of your body at all at such a time, and not being conscious of your own body, you are observing bodies outside; that's another form of objectivity.

Your mind and your emotional make-up are purer at such a time than at other times. By 'purer', I mean free from desires, impulses, etc.; you are <u>absorbed</u> in something. (Of course, this may be true in certain fields of esthetics, you understand.)

Suppose you are looking through the eyepiece of a telescope at the heavens. You are not conscious of your own body, but with a kind of impersonal intelligence, you are looking at the wonders of the heavens, the planet Saturn with its rings and moons, etc. At such a time, your mind and your heart are a little more purified than they otherwise would be, and, of course, we have these experiences in many fields. In fact, one might say that the esthetic preoccupations which we have just discussed are in a way purer than the strictly material preoccupations which we discussed at first.

Suppose you go to a symphony concert and you listen to the beauty of the music, or you see a picture, or a beautiful sunset, and you have the thought, "That is beautiful, that is lovely"; this is the esthetic intoxication itself, but nevertheless such a thought, such a feeling, is a purification, as compared to the ordinary physical passions and impulses, and it is thus easy to see that, whereas the pursuit of material happiness is apt to cause violence, killing, bloodshed, etc., the pursuit of esthetic happiness is comparatively less corrupt.

But there is something that goes higher than these. One may cultivate such a thing as the first fire. What _is_ the first fire? It is a state in which one is not engaged in pleasure-seeking of the material sort, and 'sensual' impulses are out of the way. One is not being motivated by hatred or irritability or greed at such a time, and one experiences ecstasy, which may appear in the form of skin-tingling and flashes, or waves through the body; the whole body may feel full of it, and one experiences a sense of happiness, a sense of oneness—a sense of emotional fulfilment—and one may also be thinking and reflecting at the same time. Such a condition has a peculiar property which may serve to distinguish it from other states: when one is experiencing the first fire, it is impossible to experience physical pain. We have tested this in a number of cases, and have seen that if a person is experiencing the first fire, you can pinch them so hard that you are afraid of damaging the tissue, and they will feel pressure—they are not unconscious, as if they were hypnotized -— they feel pressure, but they feel no pain. In hypnosis such a thing as not feeling pain can be suggested, but here it is not something suggested at all. You are just in the first fire, and while you are in the first fire, you do not experience pain. Of course, if you were injured in some serious way, that might bring you out of the first fire, which would be an entirely different matter. But, nevertheless—it might be said that the first fire is pure comfort, 'comfort' being defined as 'feeling no pain', and pure comfort is a very wonderful thing.

Some can go on and go into the second fire, and in the second fire the ecstasy is so intense that no I thinking or reflecting go on at all, just a vast ocean of this ecstasy, and there is a curious thing about this second fire. I mentioned that in the first fire we can experience no pain. However, we can experience unhappiness. Have you ever noticed that some moment of unhappiness, (not physical suffering, some moment of mental suffering), some moment of great grief or something of that sort, such a moment may be ecstatic in intensity? Such experiences may be of the first fire. That is why, sometimes, when we are listening to music, or seeing a motion picture or play, we are moved to weep. That is an ecstatic experience. So in the first fire, although we cannot experience pain, we can experience grief. It is a very purified and wonderful kind of grief, but nevertheless it is grief. In the second fire, grief is not possible.

In other words, in the first fire we have pure comfort, freedom from pain. In the second fire we have pure pleasure, which is free from unhappiness.

The third fire goes still further, inasmuch as the ecstasy is left behind, and one is concerned only with happiness. Ecstasy seems to be comparatively gross, and this, of course, is <u>pure</u> happiness. I may also mention that, since one has left ecstasy behind, one has also gone beyond the range of <u>pleasure</u>, one has left pleasure behind and gone on to what is just <u>pure</u> <u>happiness</u>—pleasure being a more physical sort of thing, and happiness being more mental. That is the third fire.

Now, in the fourth fire, even happiness is left behind and one experiences neither happiness or unhappiness, neither pleasure nor pain, but a feeling of oneness and a neutrality of emotion or reaction.

Let us look at these four fires again. In the first one we leave behind physical pain, in the second we leave behind mental pain or unhappiness, in the third fire we leave behind pleasure, and in the forth, we leave behind happiness. The first fire is pure <u>comfort</u>. The second fire is pure <u>pleasure</u>. The third fire is pure <u>happiness</u>. And the fourth fire is pure neutral feeling or pure <u>experiencing</u>.

These are various purifications, a series of purifications, and some people, who go through some form of integrative process, begin to experience them, and, in beginning to experience them, they discover that there is a certain satisfaction that comes from experiencing these four fires, or any one of them, and that is this: one can say to oneself, "This happiness, this realization, this attainment, is a wonderful thing, and it is an experience in which I harm no one; I do no one any harm; I do not push and shove; I am not disturbing anyone." The realization that such a happiness is possible, one which doesn't disturb anyone else and which doesn't harm anyone else, gives one a sense of satisfaction. This sense of satisfaction is what appears to be attractive about these highly intensified conditions and feelings.

What are the disadvantages connected with such wonderful experiences? Well, in the first place, they are not permanent, any more than something esthetically wonderful is permanent; our ability to attain these fire experiences may change, may age, may disappear, and therefore they have an element of dissatisfaction in them, an element of insecurity, and one should not build one's house upon such wonderful experiences. This element of dissatisfaction doesn't appear to be so very great, and yet it may well be that someone who has experienced even the first fire would feel it to be so wonderful that, if they have any reasonable amount of access to it, to lose it would cause great unhappiness. So, what is the escape; what is the way beyond; is it possible to get along without these wonderful things? Yes, it seems some people can get along quite comfortably without them; they are not preoccupied with them. That doesn't mean that they don't have them; as a matter of fact, those who are not preoccupied with them may actually have them in greater strength than others, but, by not being preoccupied with them, they have gotten rid of the disadvantages that come along with them.

These three kinds of preoccupations, these three fields, the sensual field, the esthetic field and the attainment field, are fields in which we do make changes in ourselves in the process of integration, and unless you are interested in bringing about some change in your own nature in regard to things of this sort, it is quite likely you are not very much interested in integration.

If you have certain addictions—suppose, for example, that you drink—there are many people who drink, who want to stop drinking, who would like to arrive at the condition in which they do not need to drink. There are others who drink, and intend to go on drinking for the rest of their days, and are not in the least interested in any notion of getting beyond it. Such people as are concerned with the sensual pleasure called 'drinking', and are not concerned with transforming themselves in regard to such matters, are not likely to be very much interested in integration.

There are other minor sensual pleasures that many people indulge in, such as the tobacco habit. Everybody knows that tobacco contains nicotine, which is a narcotic and generally considered to be harmful, and, whether it is harmful or not, it is certainly habit-forming. It is very easy to see how harmful it is if you watch the trembling that takes place in the person who is deprived of his nicotine for a while. Now, as long as one is going to live in the ordinary pursuit of material happiness, it doesn't make much difference whether one smokes or not, and it doesn't make much difference whether one drinks or not, as long as one doesn't drink to such an excess that it causes one to lose one's job, etc., but if one is concerned with integration, with arriving at a transformation, then it may be worthwhile to consider such addictions as the drinking habit and the smoking habit.

That doesn't mean that those who may be listening to this lecture, and who happen to have a cigarette in their hand, are expected to either give up smoking immediately or leave the room—not at all — smoking isn't necessarily given up that easily. All these people are expected to have in their minds, if they are really interested in integration, is the fact that some day, if they can manage it, they would like very much to get beyond the <u>necessity</u> of smoking, get beyond the necessity of drinking, they would like to enjoy emotional well-being, pleasure and happiness without necessarily using such devices. In other words, you should have, at least, an <u>academic</u> interest in getting beyond some of your habits, even an academic interest in getting beyond such a thing as preoccupation with sexual pursuits, or infatuation with a 'New York cut' steak, because preoccupations condition us, preoccupations with anything condition us.

I hear you thinking, "Preoccupation with integration conditions you." Yes, it does. It also is one of the preoccupations you have to get rid of on your way to complete integration. Fully integrated people are not even preoccupied with integration. They may talk a lot on the subject, but you will find that they only talk when they are asked questions, or when they are asked to go somewhere and speak on the subject. By themselves they don't talk about it, because they aren't even preoccupied with integration. There is an old saying of the teachers of integration, "To be preoccupied with anything is not to be free; not to be preoccupied with anything is to be free."

We have discussed here three kinds of preoccupation — preoccupation with material pleasure, preoccupation with mental pleasure, and preoccupation with emotional pleasure, because the physical pursuits, the sensual pursuits, are <u>physical</u> pleasure, and falling in love with this or falling in love with that is a <u>mental</u> pleasure, whether it be mathematics or a beautiful woman or a handsome man, and falling in love with these conditions of emotional excellence, these releases of the heart, these intense emotions, that is <u>emotional</u> pleasure. To get excited about any one of them leads to difficulties, and most of us are excited about one or more of these three. So integration is concerned with investigation into how best to cope with these fields—perhaps there are others—how best to cope with these three fields, and perhaps other fields, like what's the best theory of the origin of the world, what's the truth—that's another preoccupation. What's the best way to cope with such things? How is it best to live with them? Should we become transformed in our approach to them, our way of living with them, and, if so, how? That is what the field of integration is about, and, in fact, I should say that the field of integration is concerned, not with the pursuit of physical pleasure, mental pleasure, or emotional pleasure, it is not concerned with the cultivation of excellence in physical effects, the cultivation of excellence in mental associations, the cultivation of excellence in emotional attainment—it is concerned with the cultivation of <u>freedom</u> <u>from</u> <u>preoccupation</u> <u>with</u> <u>these</u> <u>things</u>.

In the field of religion, in the fields of certain forms of psycho-therapy, and in the field of certain forms of revery-therapy, there are people who become intoxicated, elated, conceited, infatuated, with one or more of these emotional attainments. To give them the benefit of the doubt, I would say that most of them become infatuated with these wonderful states called 'fire', they enjoy an exceptional emotional release which contains many of the elements of 'fire', they experience 'fire' periodically. They think this means that they have become 'perfected' or 'saved', or 'clear', as the case may be. Well, as I have mentioned, emotional attainments are all perishable. The attainments which have been called, in various walks of life, being 'saved', being 'perfected', being 'cleared', they are permanent, they are indestructible, and they do exist. They are the four degrees of integration. But these that we have been discussing are not the four degrees of integration. You can have all the fire-powers, and you may have a lot of extraordinary abilities along with them, but that does not mean you have the first degree of integration, to say nothing of the remaining three.

It is very important to realize that physical perfections, possessing this or that, possessing a wonderful body, either yours or someone else's or both, or being in love with something, dedicated to something, devoted to something or someone, or being able to enter into these wonderful attainments of fire, and knowing the purity and depth of these attainments—these things are not the first degree of integration. They are not what it means to be saved, or to be clear, or to be free, or to achieve a degree of perfection. That does not mean that the field of integration is apart from them. A person who has achieved the first, second, third or fourth degree of integration may actually possess certain physical pleasures beyond the normal range, certain mental pleasures beyond the normal range, and certain emotional pleasures like the conditions of fire, way beyond the normal range. Frequently such people have better access to these excellences, but that is not what makes them fully integrated.

Becoming fully integrated is the result of acquiring certain insights, certain understanding, and within the scope of this particular lecture, such insight, such understanding means this, to <u>know</u>, in reference to physical pleasures, the pleasures of the senses, sensual pleasures, what's the advantage of them, what's the disadvantage of them, and what's getting along without them, can it be done, and how? That's a field of insight. In regard to falling in love with this or that, or this person or that person, what's the advantage in that, what's the disadvantage and how do you get beyond it, how can you do without it, or can you? That's another kind of insight. And then in regard to these wonderful conditions of fire, emotional intensity, and sometimes the extraordinary faculties that may go along with them, what's the advantage of such things, what's the disadvantage, and is it possible to get along without them, to be unpreoccupied, to be master of them, instead of mastered by them? That's another kind of insight.

I mention this in particular, because at the present time, in the revery-therapy field, a great many people are declared to be 'clears', which is a revery-therapy term for 'saved' or 'free', and some of the people spoken of as 'clears' have indeed achieved some of the stages of fire, some of the esthetic ecstatic states. That doesn't mean they're clear. In fact, I do not know of any persons in the revery-therapy field who have, by revery-therapy methods, achieved even the first degree of integration, which in revery-therapy terms would be described as the first stage of clearness. I don't know of anyone who has done it. Because the first stage of being clear, or the first degree of integration—well, an old name for it is 'entering into the Kingdom of Heaven'—such a thing is achieved by means of <u>insight</u>, insight into such things as we have been discussing. It is <u>not</u> to be achieved simply by experiencing some of the states of fire. In fact, many of the people who have achieved such excellent releases that they have experienced conditions of fire have thereby become so elated that it is not possible to communicate with them and help them achieve the first degree of integration. They feel so wonderful that <u>what you say</u> means very little to them, but <u>what they are experiencing seems</u> 'just wonderful', and they do not realize that the very nature of what they experience and what appears to be revelation to them is very likely produced by the structuring of their own mind.

They begin to accept certain things as real—for example, many people experience 'recall' of former lives (a very common experience in many kinds of psycho-therapy). They appear to re-experience a former life. Well, <u>is</u> it a former life? Or is it something produced by some part of the mind, for some purpose? In other words, is it real, or illusory? Of course, in the therapeutic sense, we are only concerned with 'does it help?' But these people have lost that perspective, they feel so wonderful about it that they decide, "Oh, it is <u>so</u>. I <u>did</u> live in ancient Egypt", or they like the other view, and they take the attitude, "Why, that's preposterous, that's just a hallucination, all this is a snare and a delusion." When they do these things, they're <u>posing</u>, they don't really <u>know</u>, but they like the feeling of taking this stand or that stand, and thus they demonstrate that they are not 'clear', even in the first degree sense, because people who have achieved the first degree of integration do not make statements like that. They do not subscribe to any one fixed theory of life, any one fixed frame of reference, because they know that fixed theories, fixed frames of reference, are themselves limited things, and to be caught in any one of them is to have your head in a box.

So it is important to recognize that these various conditions of excellence are wonderful things, but we must have <u>insight</u> about them, not just have access to them, if we wish to become 'free', 'integrated', 'clear', 'saved', or 'enter the Kingdom'. It might be said that there are certain physical conditions of excellence, certain mental conditions of excellence, and certain emotional conditions of excellence, and a great many people throughout the world know something about them. But the only people who are achieving integration in the whole wide world are those who not only know about these three kinds of excellence, but they know what's good about them, what's bad about them, and how to get along without them, or, rather, how to get along without being preoccupied with them. In other words, <u>they</u> <u>know</u> <u>what</u> <u>is</u> <u>more</u> <u>important</u>. Only those people who know what is more important than these three kinds of excellence achieve even the first degree of integration.

In this connection I should like to quote something that was said by one of the classical authorities in the field of integration. This teacher pointed out that there are two main trends of thought in the world; one is toward materialism, and the other is toward mental- ism in various forms—it includes the idea of survival after death, as opposed to the materialist view; it includes sometimes the idea of the whole series of lives, as opposed to the materialist view—but in general you might say that one group puts matter first, and the other group puts mind first. Those are the two main streams of speculation to be found in the world, materialism and mentalism. This particular teacher of integration said, "Every teacher or philosopher who is attached, devoted, and given over to the view called materialism, is an opponent of the other school, that of the mentalist, and vice versa. Teachers and philosophers who do not know the real nature of the rise and fall of these speculative thoughts, who do not know their allure, their perils, and their outcome, these people are filled with passion, hatred, conceit, delusion, cravings and attachment, are empty of wisdom, are enemies of peace, take pleasure and delight in speculations and obsessions, and they do not arrive at a condition of full integration, freedom from unhappiness and suffering."

In short, he said that in regard to these two main trends of thought, materialism and mentalism, we must have insight about them, too; we must understand what it is that appeals to us about them, what it is that is disappointing about them, and whether it is possible to get along without them. Again, it is a matter of insight, not a matter of answering the question at all. Let's look that over for a moment. It is pretty obvious to any person who thinks about it, that materialism and mentalism are speculations. Persons who make investigations in the field, say, of survival, and who go into the field of psychical research—have you noticed that a great many of them find just exactly what they want to find? Often a man who is a confirmed materialist goes into the field of psychical research, and winds up still a confirmed materialist. Usually a person who is disposed to be a mentalist and who goes into the field of psychical research comes out a confirmed mentalist.

People who believe in survival, or believe in annihilation at death, both of them are believing just what they want to believe, and if they are very serious about it, they will realize that it is not easy, in fact it seems to be impossible, to settle these questions conclusively. This being so, why do we take up such views, why do I become a materialist, or a mentalist? Isn't the attractiveness of such a view the fact that I like to have an <u>answer</u> for things, so that I feel 'secure', so that I 'know what the facts are', or <u>think</u> I do? Now, why should I be tempted by the false security of adopting such a belief? Well, I am frightened; I am bewildered; I am confused; I want something to rely on; I want something that will give me comfort, make me feel <u>safe</u>, because I am frightened. This mystery that is my nature—I don't want to look into it without some kind of guidance, so I adopt the position of the materialist, or that of the mentalist, consider the problem solved, and don't look into my nature any more. Why? Because I have 'settled' it. If I hadn't 'settled' it, I would have to look into it more, so maybe there is an element of laziness in this, too, and certainly there is a lot of fear. So, the <u>advantage</u> of having a fixed belief of some such kind is that it gives one a sense of security, a feeling of comfort.

What is the <u>disadvantage</u>? The disadvantage appears to be that, whether either idea is the truth or not, we, by our nature, are so changing that we can't predict that we will be holding on to that idea next year, or even next week. Yesterday's materialist is apt to be tomorrow's spiritualist, and vice versa. If this is so, then there is no real security in such ideas. We are not able to hold to them any one way, because we are made of such wishy-washy material.

It may be that what this teacher of integration said is really the proper way to look at the question. There are two main trends of speculation, materialism and mentalism. And we should understand how they arise, why people take them up, what is the difficulty with them (their limitations), and whether it is possible to get free from them. That's the real problem in the field of integration.

I hope that these observations have helped you to get an understanding of what integration <u>is</u>, and what integration is <u>not</u>. I say that because to date I have heard from very few persons who hear these lectures in regard to problems concerning integration itself. I get letters from various parts of the world about E-therapy and, of course, that's well and good, but we do not achieve the first degree of integration by means of E-therapy alone; we achieve it by acquiring the type of insight that's being discussed in these talks. Therefore, if you have questions, or if you wish information on this subject, please do not hesitate to write to me. I'm very much interested in increasing the number of people who have achieved the first degree of integration. So, if you have questions on the subject of <u>insight</u>, please write to me. That is my special field.

The
Four Unthinkables

Our subject on this tape is 'The Four Unthinkables'. Now, strictly speaking, that is not a correct title. These four things which are going to be discussed on this tape are not really unthinkable; many people can and do think about them. But they are dangerous to think about; that is, thinking about them leads one into trouble. They are four things which should not be thought about - four things concerning which we should not intellectualize, theorize, speculate, 'conceptualize' about. These are four things best left alone, because speculating about them causes serious trouble and may even lead to insanity. Now, just what are these four things that we should not think about? Well, let me name them briefly. They are wise men, fire power, cause and effect and science. And in order to make clear what they really are, let us talk about them in some detail.

Why, for example, are we not to think about the nature of wise men, or integrated men, or evolved men, or whatever you want to call it? Well, suppose that a small child were to endeavor by intellectual means to try to understand the nature of a grown-up person. Might not that small child be in danger of a mental breakdown for tackling such a task? In fact, in considering the way grownups must necessarily look to small children, we can perhaps see why wise men must remain a mystery to us until the day comes when we perhaps may become a wise person. How does a grown-up person look to a child? Well, grown up people don't seem to enjoy the things that seem to be pleasurable to the child. They sometimes look on with a reminiscent or passing interest, but they don't get excited about the things that children get excited about, and, in the eyes of the child, grownups appear to lead a rather dull life, on the whole. The things that grownups really live for are not apparent to the child. All that the child notices is that the grownups don't appear to be interested in the things that seem to be really important. The grownups don't appear to take sides on questions that are vital to the child, such as which army of wooden soldiers is going to win a battle, etc. Sometimes the grownups may appear to take sides, or pretend to take sides, but they don't really care about the things that seem important to the child. Why is this? Because grownups have passed beyond the stage of being children. They have grown away from the things which interested them when they were children. They have grown beyond those things. They have grown up.

Most of us have taken the step of traveling from the state of being a child into the state of being an adult. Now, we are undertaking the journey from the state of being an adult to the state of being wise, for wise persons are grown-up adults, and we can understand how a wise person must necessarily look to us by remembering how adults look to children. That is to say, a wise man or a wise woman will look to us as if they weren't very much concerned about the things that we consider to be important. They may appear to have things which interest them, but the things which we get excited about do not excite them. The things which we consider to be of essential importance do not seem to be so regarded by the wise. So we can have no clear idea of what a wise person's interests are except to say that they are not the interests that we now have. This parallel is a very useful one to think about because it shows that just as the state of the adult is necessarily a mystery to the child, the state of the wise person is necessarily a mystery to the adult, and just as we must grow in order to become an adult, having been a child, we must also become wise in order to learn what the interests of a wise person are. Now, if we aren't content to do this, we make a serious mistake. Consider the child who has some idea as to what an adult is. He thinks that adults are cowboys or policemen or Indians or something like that - airplane pilots. If the child thinks this very seriously, if he thinks that those are really what constitute being an adult, then he is very likely to be conditioned by that, and he may grow up to become a cowboy or policeman or an Indian or an airplane pilot - not that there is anything wrong with those professions - but they may not be the child's natural calling at all. But the child may be influenced considerably by ideas about what it means to be an adult. There are many people in this world who take up smoking, or fist-fighting, or drinking, because they think that will make them adults. Now, of course, that is what they see some supposed adults doing, so they think that if they do the things that adults do, that will make them into adults.

Unfortunately, a great many people who appear to be adults aren't, really. They got into the state they are in by imitating other people who were not true adults, and so there are a great many people in the world who look like adults on the surface and physiologically they are, but mentally and emotionally they are still imitators, imitating what they thought would be an adult, and these people have never found out what it is to be adult. In the same way, suppose in our endeavor to become wise we decide to adopt in advance certain ideas about what a wise person is, what a perfected person is, a saved person, a free person. Well, if we adopt ideas about what such a person is, we will be governed by those ideas and conditioned by them, and we will grow up to be what those ideas <u>are</u>, to some degree, and we will grow to be the <u>consequences</u> of those ideas, also, in another way.

Now, by consequences, what do we mean here? Well, suppose I think that a wise person is a person who has extraordinary powers. The notion of having extraordinary powers is a very exciting one, and I may easily become excited about it, conceited about the notion of becoming a person who has extraordinary powers. Now, it appears that wise persons in some instances do really have extraordinary powers. They appear to have power over matter, extrasensory sensitivities, telepathic sensitivities, etc., and we think in our adult state - or perhaps adolescent state - we think, gee, I'd love to have power over matter and miraculous powers. Why, in no time at all I'd have Cleopatra here on a tigerskin rug and - or I'd have all the gold in Fort Knox - or I would have certain information that I've always wanted, etc. Well, we fail to realize when we speculate in that way that if we become wise to the point of having such extraordinary powers, we have at the same time become balanced, adjusted, calmed, freed from our limitations to such a degree that we no longer would want these powers for the purposes to which we would now think of putting them. That is to say, by the time we got to the point where we might have such extraordinary power as to whisk up Cleopatra on a tigerskin rug, we have found in our own resources greater pleasures than would be afforded by an interview with Cleopatra on a tigerskin rug.

I remember a young man in Honolulu to whom I once explained this. He had become quite excited about the notion of supernormal powers, and he went into a very black depression when I pointed out to him that in order to get these supernormal powers it was necessary to arrive at such a condition that these powers would not be used at all for wish fulfilment; that if they were used at all, it would simply be as a means of helping another person achieve wisdom or integration, because if I am an integrated person and you come to me, and I have only speech with which to communicate, I am somewhat limited in my ability to help you, because words are limited things. But if you come to me and I also have extrasensory faculties, I may be able to discern by means of my sensitivity just what your trouble is, and I may know how to help you more effectively. In other words, to the wise person powers are useful in perhaps the only thing that a wise person considers important, and that is helping another person become wise. But when we are just adolescents or adults not yet wise, these powers seem so exciting that many of us get all confused by pondering on them, and we get all excited about being one of the 'elect', or becoming an 'initiate' or an 'adept' or a 'master', and we speculate in various ways about the nature of wise persons, and perhaps we wind up by persuading ourselves that we <u>are</u> wise persons, and I need hardly add that if there is one thing that a wise person, a truly wise person, never thinks, it is the thought, "I am a wise person."

Now, a great deal of speculation is available in libraries and elsewhere on the subject of what wise persons are like, and if the line of reasoning which we have just gone through is true, almost every bit of this literature is dangerous and should be avoided. A large part of it goes under the name of what we call metaphysics. Metaphysics for a long time has largely consisted of speculations about what it means to be a wise person, speculations about superior orders of being, and as a game perhaps it is harmless, if we could take it as a game, but unfortunately we get very serious about it, and when we get very serious about it we not only accept some definite pattern, some definite idea as to what we will be like when we become wiser, but we neglect to take the trouble of <u>becoming</u> wiser. That is to say, we play the game of metaphysics instead of doing what we should do in order to become wiser.

Further, instead of doing what we <u>should</u> do to become wiser, we fool ourselves into thinking that we <u>are</u> doing what we should do when we are <u>not</u>. So we really go astray very badly if we speculate about what it is like to be fully integrated - in the sense of <u>speculating</u> about it and not <u>doing</u> anything about it. It is perfectly all right to spend every waking hour finding ways and means of becoming more integrated, becoming more wise, but it is not a good thing to speculate about what we will be like when we get there, because any idea we have now as to what we may be like when we get there is very apt to prevent us from getting there. It is all right to get on the train that goes to wisdom, it is all right to take a lot of trouble finding out where the railroad station is and getting on the train, but it is no good to sit at home and talk about where the train goes. That is the point which people should realize fully.

Now, some of you who listen to this discourse may be of a scientific persuasion, and you may feel something of a sense of superiority as you think of these people who speculate about superior orders of being, etc., and how foolish they are, and you may think that you have known many a crackpot who was persuaded that we live on seven spiritual planes and that there are masters, and so on and so forth, and other ideas which to you, in your eyes, are absurd. If so, sir, or madam, I should like to point out to you that the notion that there are no superior beings is also a speculation as to the nature of superior beings. That is to say, the idea that there is no such thing as an extraordinary attainment of wisdom, or freedom, or salvation, or something of that kind, is also an idea about a condition superior to this. To say that something does not exist is still to say something about it, and there is something very handy about saying that. Suppose we listen to the man who says there is an occult hierarchy and that we must become a 'neophyte' and then an 'initiate' and a 'disciple', and so on and so forth, and travel the long road to becoming a 'master'. There is a lot of work in that, and we can get out of it very easily by just denying that the whole thing exists. We can just say it isn't so, we can say we realize that when you die you are dead and there is an end to it, and all this occult twaddle is just so much nonsense, a tower of nonsense by day and a pillar of bosh by night. Well, then, of course, you who say this can feel that, "I'm about as wise as anyone, because anyone who knows the facts of life, simple materialism, that person has as much wisdom as anyone else has." So the easiest way in this world to persuade yourself that you are omniscient, that is, to have the feeling of knowing all that there is to know, is to adopt the intellectual pose of the materialist.

There is a lot less proof for the position of the materialist than there is for that of the occultist, because, as you know, there is some evidence that has been offered in favor of survival, in favor of spiritualism, in favor of telekinesis and extrasensory perception, etc. There has been evidence offered, but no one yet has brought forth evidence that when we die we go nowhere. No one yet has brought forth evidence that when we die we are <u>dead</u>, which is the belief of the materialist. The body is dead, yes, but no one has brought forth evidence that that is what we are. So the materialist is a believer in a position which has very little proof, if any, whereas the occultist is often a person who has some basis for his beliefs, although to be perfectly honest I know many, many an occultist who gets along without <u>any</u> basis for his beliefs, in so far as evidence is concerned; he has picked his beliefs because he finds them comfortable. But so has the materialist! The materialist does't have to worry about the cultivation of many virtues, the cultivation of powers that lead to wisdom, and so on, because he has just shrugged the whole thing off, and he has the advantage of looking down on everyone who believes in such nonsense, as he calls it, and that is encouraging to his conceit.

In my experience, I would say that there are two classes of persons who impress me as having more conceit in them than perhaps almost any other persons I know of, outside of a few megalomaniacs in the political sphere and in the religious sphere, that is to say, assistant professors of physics and of psychology, such as we find in the universities. We find that full professors of physics and of psychology have a certain amount of humility. They know their subjects well enough to know that there are a great many things that they don't know. Quite frequently they are open-minded persons. But assistant professors often haven't learned this yet, and they have an air of smug conceit, smug self-satisfaction about them that is quite a remarkable thing to behold, and of course it prevents any integration of the personality as long as it lasts, and it may even cause them to become extraordinarily poorly adjusted persons in their daily life.

So if you have a scientific background and have had various pressures put upon you to turn you into a materialist, let me point out that materialism is also a speculation about what a wise man is. To say that there is no such thing as a wise man or a wise man is one who knows chemistry and physics better than other people, and so on, to say that is to have a definite view about what a wise man is. Now, I am not saying that materialism isn't so. It may be so. It seems to me that one of the things we have to learn on the way to wisdom is to live our lives in such a way that no matter what theory of reality may be the truth, we live intelligently even according to that theory. Now, if we persuade ourselves that we know that materialism is true or that it is untrue, we may be pretending to know something that we do not really know, and to pretend to know something that we do not really know is a form of conceit, and conceit is such a self-satisfying thing that it often prevents the intelligent functioning of the mind for long periods, so be on your guard against anything which you find flattering to your own ego, to your own individuality, personality. Such things can immobilize you, mentally, transformationally, for quite some time.

Now, the second item on our list of things not to think about, not to speculate about, is fire power. Now, what do we mean by fire power? Well, at various times in our lives

43

we have felt extraordinary intensity of pleasure or of happiness. Sometimes this is felt in the sexual experience, sometimes in esthetic experiences, like listening to a wonderful symphony, or watching a sunset, seeing a waterfall, sometimes in moments of personal relationship, or even in moments of grief, these intense experiences are attained. Some people enjoy such an extraordinarily well-equipped endocrine system, nervous system, that they have ecstatic experiences frequently, and people who have these ecstatic experiences frequently, these experiences of fire - 'fire' being simply a name for emotional intensity - people who have these fire experiences frequently are apt to discover that many supernormal powers go along with them, such as extrasensory perception, healing, and so on.

There is abroad in this country at the present time a teaching called 'Tono-Therapy'. I've forgotten the name of the man who originated it now, back in Pittsburgh - 'Tono-Therapy' by Jack Beever - it comes back to me, and the basic teaching of 'Tono-Therapy' is - station your mind, your consciousness, your center of consciousness, say, oh, on one of the tips of your fingers - the tip of your finger - station your attention there for a while, and perhaps you will discover after a bit that there appears to be a vibration or a buzzing or an energy intensity there, and just let your consciousness stay in this spot, and this intensity may grow and become quite an ecstatic or pleasurable thing. Of course, this is a way of making fire in a certain part of the body, and some people can do it. Now, the curious thing is that - suppose you have, say, an infection on the back of your hand. Well, you might pick a knuckle right near that infection which is not infected and proceed to generate fire, this intensified feeling, in that one knuckle - assuming that you are one of those people who can do this - and then cause the area of the fire-feeling to spread until it comes to the infected area, and if you can cause the fire-feeling to spread through the infected area, you will very likely have either an instantaneous or a rapid healing. Such is the power of the fire experience. Now, doctors have a name for it. They call it 'euphoria', and many people who experience euphoria are so carried away by it that they are not able to tend to their ordinary affairs and so they are locked up in an asylum. But it is not so much that they are insane as that they are having an experience which preoccupies them so that they just haven't time to tend to normal business. There are many people who are called 'elated' persons in asylums who are quite pleasant to talk to, but they get so absorbed in certain things which they are enjoying that they really aren't safe to be allowed out, so they are kept locked up.

Now, this whole idea of extraordinary powers is one about which there are many speculations, pro and con, and it seems to be a very vast subject in that the nature of the powers appears to be very vast. It has been discovered in the field of psychotherapy that apparently it is possible to do healing over great distances of many thousands of miles by means of certain methods of extraordinary energy transfer, or whatever you want to call it. Now, some people get excited about this subject. They want to speculate about the existence of fire power or extrasensory power (occult power, if you like), because it is certainly not the obvious external type of power, and they speculate endlessly about these subjects. I mean to say that I have found individuals - actually met them and talked to them and seen their libraries - individuals who have collected vast libraries on psychical research. It never occurred to them to try to experiment themselves and find out what they could experience along those lines. They just collected a library and have been collecting ideas about the subject of psychical research, ideas as to whether mediumship is possible and whether survival is possible and so forth and so on. There are others who have collected libraries on Yoga. I myself was one of those once. I practised Yoga at various times in my life, but it is true I read a great deal more about it than I ever practised, and for many years I spent a great deal of time reading on the subject of these extraordinary abilities, and also on the first subject mentioned, the nature of the wise man. It is true - perhaps the thing that kept me moderately sane - if, indeed, I can be so characterized - was the fact that I was looking into all these things with the object of <u>doing</u> something about them. I was very much interested in the notion of how to become wise or wiser. I was interested, in a kind of passing way, in the notion of extraordinary powers. I never got too excited about wanting to have them, and, in fact, on one occasion when I took what we call a 'psychochemical', mescaline, I was in a state where many of my natural impulses were free to express themselves. I seemed to have no inclination toward supernormal faculties of any kind. I simply wanted a release of the heart, whatever that means. So I didn't have a motivation to get excited about extraordinary powers. I did have a tremendous and absorbing interest in what a wise man is, but it was the kind of interest that goes along with the basic question of - how does one get there? Now I know that I did go through a period when I thought that - gee, someday I'll be a wise man of such and such a type and that will be an exalted condition and people will think I'm important and so on and so forth. But, by and by, in the process of acquiring even a little bit of wisdom, one gets beyond all such speculations, all such ego projections, and simply discovers that wisdom, when one arrives there, consists in living from day to day, or, as an old saying goes, 'sleeping when tired, eating when hungry', that is to say, that the wisdom that is attained as a result of seeking wisdom in whatever is the effective way, that wisdom consists in living simply and directly and openly and naturally. It sounds easy to say it, but it isn't really. It is not an easy thing to attain, nor is it by any means an easy thing to express. But the wise person in many ways is simpler, less complex, than the person who has not achieved wisdom, and I am not sure that that statement should be allowed, because here we are warning against speculating about the nature of the wise man, and here I am doing just such speculating, certainly not very smart, and in case any person has the notion that I have arrived at the state of being a wise person, why there is the evidence to the contrary. Well, extraordinary powers, pros and cons of psychical research and so on, they are not things to be thought about because they also can condition us, and, again, let me say to our scientific friends that notions of the materialistic sort to the effect that these powers and faculties do not exist are also speculations about them, and such speculations can close the mind, can cramp the mind and can cause conceit just as much as speculations about the nonexistence of wisdom, and so on and so forth. So speculating about the nature of the superior person, speculating about the powers of the superior person, are at the very least a waste of time, and there are many people in our asylums who got there by speculating about these things. Now, of course, again, let me point out that what we call 'metaphysics' is largely a collection of speculations about these two subjects, and metaphysics, therefore, is for the most part a waste of time, and, again, let me say that what is called orthodox scientific materialism is a metaphysics. It is a definite set of views about these things, and therefore it also is a waste of time.

Now, our third subject with a 'Keep Off The Grass' sign is the subject of cause and effect, what in the Orient and among Theosophists, etc., is called 'karma'. It is a very, very complicated subject, one we should not speculate upon because it becomes too complicated for the reach of the mind. In the first place, some people when they talk about 'karma' talk about the old Mosaic Law, an eye for an eye, a tooth for a tooth, and that gets into our whole system of legal procedure, crime and punishment, which is a very complicated field. Then there are others who when they talk about 'karma' speak about former lives, and it does appear that in about one-third of all cases who undergo certain forms of psychotherapy, that people do seem to re-experience what appears to be former lives. Maybe they are and maybe they aren't; maybe they are produced by a scenario-writing-and-producing department of the mind, but in any event they do appear, and the question is that when some person undergoing psychotherapy experiences what appears to be having lived a life in ancient Greece, what is the connection; what is the 'karma'; what is the cause and effect of such a thing as that; how is it connected with the person here in this life? Is it something that has come out of this present mind, or is it something that really came down from the ancient past? Again, if we appear to experience something that comes apparently from the ancient past, is it really ours? Are we connected with it? Or is it that there is a universal mind that has recorded everything and we just tune in upon it, or is it someone else's experience, someone that we have no direct contact with? What is the connection? One can speculate a great deal about that, and there is many a metaphysical book that is filled with notions of 'karma' and reincarnation, etc.

Now, then, again, here is another problem: You and I are separate in some respects, that is to say, the voice that you hear proceeds from what is described as a male body about 73 inches tall and weighing about 230 pounds - which is, I believe, about 35 pounds more than it should weigh - and you who listen have a body of other dimensions, for the most part. Some of you may be of just that same size. So these bodies are separate. Your body eats and sleeps in one place, and my body eats and sleeps in another place, and, if you have been listening just to this tape, we have been exchanging - well, not exactly exchanging - but let's say you have been receiving certain thoughts and feelings from this personality, and if you and I are acquainted and have had any correspondence, why there has been an exchange, too. I have received certain thoughts and feelings from you. Now, if that has been going on for any length of time, even 10 minutes, who is to say where you begin and I leave off, and vice versa? The boundary line between us is not so easy to state as it is physically, for you may be at one end of the country and I may be at another, physically, but in this process that is going on right now, let us suppose that you are an individual some distance from me; you do not know me personally, perhaps have never seen me - not that that is any great loss - but let us suppose that we are strangers except insofar as these tapes are concerned. Now, when you listen to this voice that comes to you from a tape recorder or playback machine, this voice - well, you hear it in your mind - we don't know really what the sound waves are like in this room. They are just sound waves, but these sound waves come from the machine. They enter your ear, your ear translates it into certain nervous stimuli, and then in the mind this voice appears, that is, this voice of mine which at the moment appears to me to come from my mouth here, whatever that means - there really is in you a voice in your mind, and this voice in your mind to some degree carries your thinking along with it. To some degree your thinking may go in other directions, but nevertheless there is a flowing there, and to some degree these words are part of your thinking. That being so, are we so all-fired separate? Are we really distinct? Am I one person and you another? And are we separate so far as action and reaction, cause and effect, is concerned? Well, you can see it is a complicated subject, and if one were inclined to speculate about cause and effect, about responsibility for action, one could really get awfully complicated about it, and there are metaphysical books and teachings about this same subject. There are metaphysical books that are called metaphysical books, and there are metaphysical books that are called law books, because I can assure you that our law books contain a system of metaphysics, definite beliefs about what a person is, which may or may not be correct.

I know of a young man who got out of a mental asylum a couple of years ago by means of people who worked some 20 miles away from him relieving his tensions, and he responded at the same time that they gave the treatment, on several occasions. There is very little doubt that he was helped in just that way and at just those times. These people would lie down and relax and ask their upstairs minds, if you like, to relieve that young man's tensions through them, and then they would feel aches and pains, and so on and so forth, and he apparently was relieved. I don't know whether I have recorded on tape an account of that particular incident or not. I believe that it is discussed - it may be discussed in my tape No. 17 called 'How War Will End', but I am not certain. Well, no matter. The point is that if I wish to help someone who is in an asylum - since I have no medical degree, in fact no official licensing of any kind, I am not allowed by law to go into this asylum and help this individual, but if I sit at home and do what we call 'proxy', experience his tensions for him and release them, act as a drainpipe for him, according to our metaphysics in the law courts, no court of law would consider that I had actually given this person treatment. That is, if the doctor of this patient were to suspect that I were influencing the patient at a distance, he wouldn't have any luck in the world if he went to court to try to sue me, to claim that I had tampered with the patient in the asylum. So the legal system has its own metaphysics, its own beliefs about cause and effect, and to think, to muse, about cause and effect - it is such an intricate subject. And since identities are so hard to establish, the identity of you, the identity of me, that is something that is just as well to leave alone. That is something - it is an entire field which has a sign on it that says 'Keep Off The Grass'. And there are people in our asylums, and there are people in many of our religious sects, who have exaggerated notions about cause and effect, of what is a crime and what is a punishment, and so forth. In other words, when people go crazy, they generally go crazy about these things: What is a superior being? What is an extraordinary power? What is a crime? Or a meritorious action? These are dangerous fields.

Now, of course, many of us have to have some kind of working grasp in these fields in order to get along in our daily lives. It is not that the subjects are taboo. Certainly the man who is a lawyer by profession has to know something of the law code; the man who is a judge and so on and so forth has to know something about these things. But that is not the same as being preoccupied by them and getting overly excited about them; it is quite a different thing. Our main business in this world is to become integrated, to learn to live directly and simply instead of in a fragmentary and disintegrated manner, and that is what we should put our time to. That is, we should get on the train that goes to wisdom. We shouldn't sit here and speculate about where the train is going, what power drives it, and just exactly what rules govern its operation, which is what these three speculations amount to.

There is still another speculation, and that is what is the countryside like through which the train goes? We might sit at home and speculate about that. The important thing is to go get on the train and make the journey. Now, what does it mean to speculate about the countryside? Well, that is the last of our speculations of these four, and it is called science, and it has to do with this kind of thing: What is the moon? What is the sun? What is an eclipse of the moon? Why do plants grow? Why do trees have roots? - all those questions which are usually taken up by science. Now, in our daily life we may have reason to learn certain of these things.

But I am speaking now of the people who have made science a preoccupation, not necessarily a profession, because many a professional scientist or engineer is still a healthy and fairly well-balanced man outside of his profession - but I am speaking of the people who get an insatiate urge to learn all about everything. I had that urge for a long period of years - oh, I wouldn't say all about everything - there were certain fields in which I had very little interest - but I had to learn all about electronics, physical and mathematical science, at the very least. I had to learn all about music in a certain way, about writing and history, certain fields of history, and so on. Well, that can be a preoccupation, that can be a strong conditioning factor. It can be something that one gets lost in, gets wound up in, gets perplexed in. It can be something that one goes crazy over.

For example, I speculated for years on what is called the theory of numbers, questions like - what is and what is not a prime number, or a perfect number, and so on. There are people who have been locked up because they just 'lost their marbles', as the saying goes, playing such games, trying to find out what is a means of testing numbers to determine whether any number will divide into them or not. The number you can't divide is a prime number, and I guess you all know what they are - 2, 3, 5, 7, 11 and 13 and so on are numbers that can't be divided by any whole number other than one and themselves, and they are prime numbers. Other numbers like 15 are made up of prime numbers, 3 x 5, and so on. It is quite a problem to determine whether a large number like 4181 - whether that is a prime number or not. Well, I beat my brains out for years trying to do just such things. I agitated myself - still do to some degree occasionally - and there are people who have really gotten in such a state that they were candidates for a butterfly net and had to be taken away to special homes where they could be provided for. So in becoming preoccupied with some particular field of science or learning - I don't just mean science alone - some field of learning, even such a thing as collecting stamps - some people quite lose their balance on such a subject.

So we have four basic fields of preoccupation, four general types of preoccupation which if practised to any excessive degree - even to any very great degree - can seriously disturb the mind, can obstruct the integrative process and can cause us to neglect the integrative process, which is what we are really here for, and those four things are speculating about what a superior person is, speculating about what extraordinary powers are, speculating about cause and effect, crime and punishment, guilt and innocence, and speculating about the nature of things, the nature of things mind you, in an inorganic sense, in the sense of just piling up information. Of course, in the process of becoming integrated we do have to speculate very deeply, and, in speculating, we have to look very deeply into the nature of what we are and what is around us. We have to look into that very deeply, but that is not a process of learning, it is not a process of gathering information and labeling it in concepts and ideas, conceptions of things. As we become integrated we learn to look at things more and think about things less. We learn to experience more and theorize less, or realize more and theorize less, but intellectualizing, for the most part, is of these four kinds. I don't know whether they are four all-inclusive types of intellectualizing. I don't know that I would say definitely that they are. For example, there is another kind of intellectualizing I can think of called 'conventionalizing'. There are people who do quite well in this world simply because they store up information as to just what is done and what is not done. That is the only kind of thinking they do. They 'convench', I used to say. They conventionalize. And then there are men who make a pile of money because they never do anything but 'figure'. They 'figure' what to do. They scheme, they plan, they 'figure' all the time mentally, and some of them are very successful at it, make a lot of money, but they still don't use their minds for anything but 'figuring'.

Well, now those two types of activity - I don't know that they come under the general heading of these four that I have mentioned. I can see perhaps why not, and that is that a person who is very conventional is in a way trying to adjust to the community life, and a person who 'figures' is trying to adjust to conditions as they are in the external world. Therefore, such people are more apt to remain what we call 'sane' and able to get around and do things than are people who take up these other preoccupations. The scientist, for example, is well known to be an absentminded character, or at least thought of to be that. Most scientists that are worthy of the name are better balanced than we might suspect, but nevertheless the man who becomes too preoccupied with his field of learning, or art, is apt to be the 'absent-minded' professor. And people who get preoccupied with metaphysics certainly do get out of touch with life around them, so they are much more likely to be locked up, to get out of adjustment with the external world into a condition that we call 'insanity'. I think that it is very good to realize that these four different fields of mental exercise or gymnastics are dangerous and should be avoided as much as possible.

The first is - let us not speculate or try to find out in advance what we will be like when we become wiser. Let us content ourselves with just becoming wiser, to the best of our ability. Second, do not let us speculate what extraordinary powers are. Let us work in the direction of them if we wish, or observe what there are that we have, or let the subject alone, one or the other; let's not speculate as to what they are or are not. Remember that the negative speculations are bad, too. The third - let us not speculate as to what is right and what is wrong and what is true and false and what is crime and punishment, what is cause and what is effect The mechanism of life is very, very complicated, and it is best not to try to make any intellectual explanation of what it is all about. It is much better to watch our own actions as we see them and as much as we see of them and let the harmonizing process take place in us as we do that. And then the last one is - let us not get too excited about any form of information. Let us not make a mountain of our learning in any subject. For example, I have a mountain of learning which I really don't need, which I have piled up over a period of years. I imagine that I could recognize any one of 100 or more symphonies if almost any part of the symphony were played for me. There is quite a number of them I could probably wave my arms convincingly enough to conduct. Well, why? - simply because I listened to them a great many times, and that would be a pile of learning that I piled up. I don't need it now. I used to think that it wasn't possible for me to endure daily life unless I listened to a great and wonderful symphony or read a wonderful book, or something like that, and now I am beginning to discover that very simple things are wonderful symphonies and wonderful books, so that that particular pile of learning that I had is not so exciting as it once was.

Now, you may say - well, certainly we shouldn't go through life without any ideas on these four subjects. Well, of course not. I would say that so far as the fourth one is concerned - general information - we certainly should have enough general information to be an intelligent citizen and be able to earn our living. As far as the other three are concerned, a very good guide as to how much we should know about them would be this: Consider the classical authorities and learn as much as they teach - no more. That is to say, the classical authorities, the great teachers of integration that the world has seen - who are they? Well, there is the Rishi Kapila, 1250 B.C.; there was Sri Krishna, 750 B.C.; there was Lao Tzu, about 600 B.C.; there was Gautama Buddha, 559 to 475 B.0.; there was Jesus of Nazareth, about 4 B.C. to 29 A.D. are his correct dates. There is Mr. Krishnamurti, born in 1895 and still living as of this date, 1954. Now, those appear to be the primary authorities in the field of integration. Each one has a different approach. If you study the Buddha, for example, you will find quite a little bit of discussion of the different degrees of integration, and so on. If you study the work of Mr. Krishnamurti, you will find very little discussion of it. But nevertheless, even in the case of the Buddha, things are not gone into in excessive detail - just enough to tell us what the direction of integration is, and not enough to tell us what we seem to want answers for when we speculate in these various fields.

And then it occurs to me that there is another thought behind this idea that there are four unthinkables, four things not to think about, and that is that in the last analysis, they really are <u>unthinkable</u>. That is, the nature of the wise man is unthinkable because the wise man is a person who has learned to live so directly that he is not describable in terms of a pattern of thought; he is spontaneous, and cannot be described in terms of a definite pattern. Likewise, perhaps, the occult powers, the fire powers, may be so wonderful, and so four-dimensional, if you like, that we cannot really describe them. We cannot get a perfect intellectual description of what they are. Perhaps some day we might get a mathematical description, and maybe not, and the same is true with cause and effect Perhaps it is so complicated a subject that some new and strange tensor calculus is necessary in order to tackle it, and therefore the mind is not capable of satisfying itself in an intellectual collection of concepts which describe cause and effect exactly. The same may be true with science. Maybe the perfect science is unattainable, and yet the intellect wants to find the perfect science, and therefore it is a kind of fruitless quest.

In general, instead of trying to get an intellectual grasp of things, what we should do is enter into direct relationship with things, and perhaps that is the real lesson behind the study of these four unthinkables. After all, thinking about something is only a substitute for experiencing it, and actually I've tried a little bit of both, and it's been my experience that thinking, trying to grasp the nature of reality by means of thinking, by intellectualizing, is much harder work than grasping it by growing into it. It's really much more trouble than it is worth. It is a waste of time in several ways. That is to say, by the time you could get intellectually a clear conception of what highly integrated persons are, a reasonably clear conception, by that time you could have become one several times over. You can spend years and years and years studying how fully integrated persons act and talk, etc., but, according to the classical authorities, if you apply yourself properly, you can, in any length of time from several years down to several days, become one. The differences in time required depend on your own aptitude, but seven years at the outside, and many of us have spent several times seven years just reading up on the subject. So it is a good thing to think, if we are going to think at all, that realizing is more important than theorizing, that experiencing is more important than speculating, and that speculating on certain subjects can lead to serious trouble, and delay, and possibly insanity.

The Easiest Way

Many people have asked me, "What's the easiest way to get people started in integrative work?" Well, it isn't always easy to start people off in an E-Therapy session, for example, because it doesn't work for everyone. Those it works for — that's fine, but there're a lot of people that aren't going to lie down and let you commence therapy. They're not going to get that far — they're not going to take that much interest in it. But you can get almost anyone to come sit in a group - just to see what's going on. They don't have to commit themselves in any way at all.

And this method I'm going to tell you about is a method which can be used in a group. You can bring a person to that group who knows nothing whatever about it, and he may be the star performer of the group before the evening is over. Nobody will have to push him or anything. So, it's something that you can try. Furthermore, it's something that you can try if you're a whole group of people that don't know <u>beans</u> about E-Therapy — never tried it. It's something that you can start right from <u>scratch</u>.

Now, I mention the name 'E-Therapy'. Well, what on earth is E-Therapy? E-Therapy might be described as a kind of psychological vomiting. Suppose you eat something that's poisonous - your system causes you to vomit — throw it up — get it out of your system. A lot of us, in many ways, have had experiences that we can't digest — and E-Therapy is a way of getting them out of the system.

What is 'E'? It seems that the psychologists have taught that we have an ordinary mind and a subconscious mind. The ordinary mind is a kind of street-level mind, and the subconscious mind is a kind of downstairs mind. And most all of us know about that. The downstairs mind is supposed to contain a lot of leftover trash from yesterday that bothers us. Some of the psychologists have suggested that there's an upstairs mind, too. And this upstairs mind knows a lot more than the normal street-level mind. In some people, called 'prodigies', it peeks through.

Consider this for a moment. Consider that we're all geniuses — that is — we have a genius mind upstairs, but that in most of us, it's not connected. In most of us, only the street-level mind is connected. Now it isn't hard to just consider that possibility. And that's all you're asked to do - just sort of play along with it. Let's pretend that that's so for a while. And if you do that, you'll find that some amazing things will happen. You don't have to believe it — just pretend. Because it's very easy to get these upstairs minds to show themselves. We call them 'E' — for short.

So, if you have a group of people, and you want to try out this easy approach to integrative work, this therapy, just ask them all to <u>suppose</u> that they have an upstairs mind, of which they're normally not conscious and that this upstairs mind has many wondrous abilities — all kinds of wondrous abilities - which the street level or normal mind doesn't know anything about. And then just ask the group this: "Now, let's all ask our 'E's — our upstairs minds — to prepare us for a Group-E session — and let's devote three minutes to this." And ask the people just to sit there for three minutes and watch and see what happens in their own persons. Some of them may feel something; watch and see how the upstairs mind may communicate. So, everyone is quiet for three minutes. At the end of that time you can say, "Well, how is everybody's 'E' tonight?"

You'll find that some people report that during that three minutes time, they were surprised to discover that they didn't do any thinking at all, that their mind was just perfectly blank. Others will report that they felt a pleasant tingling, or had some wonderful experience, like seeing a beautiful color. Others will report that they trembled, or had a tendency to shake. And others may report that they felt an uncontrollable impulse to move this or that part of the body, make faces, or something. Still others will report that they felt an ache or pain here or there, or they suddenly seemed to remember something that happened a long time before; or that they saw a symbol of some kind in their mind. All kinds of things may be reported.

Well, you're off now! You've asked these people to pretend that there's an upstairs mind that knows a whole lot of things and has a lot of special abilities. And you've asked those upstairs minds, those 'E's, to get everybody ready for a Group-E session and devoted three minutes to it. Now what do you do? Whoever is the leader of the group — he doesn't do any extraordinary amount of magic — he simply is the mouthpiece of the group — he then says, "Now, is there anybody present who has an ache or a pain?"

Some lady, say Mrs. Jones, may speak up and say, "Well, I've had a terrible headache lately. I have it now." So the leader of the group replies, "Let us ask our 'E's to work on the problem of Mrs. Jones' headache. Let us authorize our 'E's to take energy from us and give it to her, if that will help. Let us authorize our 'E' so to take tensions from her and release them through us, to the extent that that can be done safely, if that will help. Or let us ask our 'E's to give us information in various ways that may help Mrs. Jones."

Now everybody sits back and watches within his own person to see what happens. A couple of people may report they feel a headache. Of course, that may be due to suggestion, from Mrs. Jones having mentioned a headache, or it might be something else. We don't know. It doesn't matter, because it's going to make Mrs. Jones feel better to know that some people are at least concentrating their attention, in some way, on her problem.

Somebody else may speak up and say, "I have an ache in my elbow." Or, "I feel a pain in my stomach", and so on. People will feel different things. Some other people will just be blank, and not appear to take much part in it. Maybe they're giving energy, and don't know it. Some others may feel a pleasant tingling in different parts of the body. And — not necessarily in every group — but in some groups - some of them may say to Mrs. Jones, "I see you in an automobile accident. I see that you have had your skull fractured in an automobile accident. I see you thrown clear of the car, and your headache comes from the shock of that accident." Mrs. Jones may say, "Why, yes, how did you know?" And the other party, who may be a perfect stranger to Mrs. Jones, may say, "I don't know — I just got mental pictures of the incident."

You'll find that a number of things like that do happen in groups, and that's where it gets out of the range of just suggestion. Naturally, Mrs. Jones is going to feel a little better if everybody there asks his 'E' — whatever that may be — to work on her headache. It's comforting to know that other people are interested in your welfare. But when people begin to get material that seems to be in great detail, and can, for example, report an auto accident that you were in, and somebody else feels a pain in the elbow and it turns out you were hurt in the elbow, too, there may be something operating here that's a little out of the ordinary.

So, Mrs. Jones may report that after two or three minutes or so, her headache is gone. She may not. But just let people go on reporting what they experience. In our experience, I would say that in nine cases out of ten, the headache will be gone. Let the material keep coming, let it keep flowing for a while. Now, the leader can then go on and say, "Is there any other person present who has an ache or a pain?"

Let's say that Mr. Johnson remarks, "Yes. I've had a kind of fever for several days now, and I'd appreciate it if you could help me." Now, mind you, Mr. Johnson may not believe in this. He may think it's some kind of faith-healing cult. But he's willing to take a chance, because he'd like to get rid of his fever. The leader then says, "All right, let's all ask our 'E's to take up the problem of Mr. Johnson's fever."

Immediately, a certain number of people present will begin to report that they feel this or that, or that they have a tingling or pleasant experience of some kind, or there may be a pain. Some of the others will remain quiet, neutral, and some others may get definite pictures or information about Mr. Johnson's background — what may be the cause of this trouble. Three or four minutes go by and perhaps Mr. Johnson's fever has stopped. It very frequently happens that way.

The leader then takes up someone else's problem. When he has used up one-third to one-half of the time available for the meeting (you don't necessarily spend more than about five minutes on any one person) he can say if he wishes, "Is there any person present who has been trying to get better E-contact?" Let's say Jim Smith speaks up and says, "Yes, I've been trying E-Therapy for some time, and I don't seem to get good results. I'd like some help." The group is then directed to ask their 'E's to work on Jim Smith's case and help him get in better contact with his 'E'. Immediately, some of the group begin to feel this or that, tingling, pain, pleasant sensations. Somebody else may get a phrase. They may say, "I get the phrase, 'I don't need any help from anybody.'" The leader may say to Jim Smith, "Do you remember ever saying that?" Jim says, "Well, I'm not sure — I may have said that at one time or another in my life." So the leader says, "Repeat that phrase for a while, in case it does have some effect on you. We can perhaps bring it to the surface."

Jim then starts repeating, "I don't need any help from anybody," several times, as politely as he can, though mentally he may think everybody there is crazy. But he repeats it, and then, after awhile, perhaps the person who got the idea of the phrase, speaks up and says, "I think that's enough." Or, the leader may make that suggestion. After five or ten minutes, nothing may appear to be accomplished; on the other hand, sometimes Jim Smith's case will have been opened wide.

The leader goes on to someone else. "Does someone else want better contact with his 'E'?" And they all try again. You can keep this up until practically everyone in the group is taken care of, depending on the size of the group, or you can take only those who volunteer.

That is what is called 'Group-E'. Group-E can be done by people who have never had an E-session, people who know very little about it. There are certain things that have to be considered by the leader in Group-E work. One thing to remember is this: Don't try to conduct the therapy yourself. The 'E's are doing it — whatever the 'E's may be. You are simply to keep the group working as a unit, but you leave it up to the 'E's as to what's being done. You really don't have to know anything much to be a leader of the group. You simply have to be willing to operate on the premise, for the time being, that the 'E's know what to do and they'll take care of it. It might help if the leader is familiar with the E-Therapy book and has some idea of what 'E's are all about. Maybe the leader has done some therapy. But it's not so terribly important. You <u>can</u> start from scratch and do it.

One thing I'd like to mention. Suppose that Jim Smith has some problem which it would not be nice to bring out in the presence of a group, and yet that problem may be part of what we asked for in helping him get better contact with his 'E'. These 'E's are extraordinarily tactful. Someone may say, "I see a picture of a pedestal." The leader may say, "What does that mean?" He may turn to Jim Smith and say, "Does that mean anything to you?" Jim says, "No." The person that saw the picture says, "I get the impression that he puts something on a pedestal." That may mean that he worships his mother-in-law, or his father, or the American way of life, or something else. The point is that the 'E's in charge do not want to state it in so many words, so they bring it out in a symbol. The leader must remember not to try to inquire into what it means. Rather, he should do this: He can say, "Now, if putting something on a pedestal is connected with

Jim's case, let us ask the 'E's present if they will attack this problem and solve it."

After a while maybe there will be a report from the person who saw the pedestal, something as follows: "I see the pedestal tipping over to one side - it's slowly tipping." He may get a progress report, and say pretty soon, "It has fallen over." Then the leader can assume that whatever Jim's problem was has been relieved by the joint energy of all the 'E's present. He may say, "We don't know what it was, but we got the picture, and apparently something was done." So it's important to remember that the 'E's will protect any person's privacy; nobody has to worry about indiscreet statements coming out in a Group-E session. The 'E's know what they are doing.

This sounds a bit crazy, I know. But you try it, and you will find that the people who attend these group meetings begin to have things happen to them. They begin to be transformed; they get rid of some of their problems There are people who report that they have been cured of cancers, tumors, deafness, etc., by attendance at just such groups. To be sure, it's a kind of a healing group, in a way, but it doesn't involve faith. Many people get faith in the activity of the 'E's. But you don't have to believe in the 'E's to get results. It merely involves a simple willingness to just play ball for a while, and to just pretend that there is a mind in us called 'E' and these 'E's are all sort of like guardian angels who will help do the work. You don't have to believe in angels; you don't have to believe in spirits; you don't have to believe in God; you don't have to believe in anything: just <u>try</u> it. Even if you are a hardboiled materialist, you'll admit that we don't know all about the ninety-five percent of the brain that scientists say isn't being used. Maybe this ninety-five percent of the brain has the power to do some of these strange things. Maybe we don't know what really happens in a Group-E session. The most important thing about it is that it happens.

So, if you want to start a Group-E session, do it more or less along the lines indicated here. If you want to, at the end you can say as your last request, "Now, let's ask the 'E's to mop up whatever tensions may be left over in this group, as a result of this work." And take a couple of minutes for that, and then you're through.

Bear in mind that this work is something that isn't done in the dark - although it may be advantageous to subdue the lights a little bit for the benefit of those who see pictures. There's nothing hocus pocus about it; you're not going through any involved ritual. You're just making one simple assumption - that each person there has a super-mind attached, and that this super-mind can do wonderful things, if asked to do them. It is only an assumption. Then watch to see what happens.

Now, let's go into some detail as to what you, as an individual, can do to help in Group-E work. I want to do this because a great many people are learning to make quite an art of this, and it's a good idea to talk about just exactly what does happen. I've already mentioned several groupings. There's the leader who sometimes asks questions. Sometimes another person will ask a pertinent question, but it may get confusing, so it's better for the leader himself to do it. The leader asks questions; that's his job, to try to figure out what's the right question to ask (if he's going to ask any).

Then there are the people who answer the questions. Then there are people who give energy. There are those who release tensions. That's four groupings. We'll talk more about them later.

But let's go into a little more detail. In the first place, if Mrs. Jones has a headache and the leader says, "Now, let us ask our 'E's to help Mrs. Jones' headache," that's asking, isn't it? Asking is the first step in E Therapy. Now some people can ask better than others. If you have a good disposition toward people and would like to see Mrs. Jones helped, join the leader in the asking - not out loud - but ask in your heart sincerely, "Please, 'E's present, help Mrs. Jones with her headache." You're helping with asking, then. That may be your contribution to the Group-E.

You may also have a tendency to go into what we call 'turn-off'. Your mind becomes very quiet. You're hearing what's going on, but you're not thinking at all. You're in a very receptive, quiet state, like a camera that has its shutter open to take a picture - quiet and receptive. All right, if 'turn-off' is something that you are engaged in, that is your contribution, because resting in that quiet state seems to be the best way of standing at attention in the presence of an 'E', so to speak. You are putting yourself at the service of 'E', if you can rest in that quiet state.

Again, you may experience the tingling and flashes, etc., of fire energy. That means that 'E' is stirring up fire energy in you that may be transmitted to these other people, and if you feel such energy being stirred up in you and it's not your turn - that is, you're not being worked on - or if you feel any other kind of energy, or if you have reason to suspect that your energy is being used — then ask, "May this energy be used to help Mrs. Jones, or to help the 'E's in their work?" You can ask that specifically, if you like, because some people seem to be able to give energy to the 'E's. So, if you have fire energy in you — fire being the name we use for ecstatic energy, emotional-intensity energy, physiological ecstasy — let the 'E's have it. And even if you don't have that, but just have ordinary nervous energy, just say to yourself, or to your 'E', "Please use such energy as you need from me to help Mrs. Jones," and make yourself available with that thought.

If you have a tendency to tremble or shake in an E session, or feel a tendency to tremble and shake, that means that some of Mrs. Jones' tensions are coming out through you. Go ahead and shake! You will look a little foolish, but I swear this whole business looks foolish, and in fact, in many a Group-E session there is a lot of laughing going on because of the various things that happen. But it works just the same, and laughing doesn't hurt it. So, if you have to shake, and your arms appear to shake off, or your legs, why, go right ahead. Just shake!

And, again, you may have a tendency to want to twist your head around, or make faces, or squint, or go through the motions of fist fighting, or something; you may feel all kinds of tensions moving you. To the extent that you can do that without injuring your neighbor, go right ahead! That's the way of releasing tensions. This may be your contribution.

Then, there's also the possibility that you may experience definite pains in different parts of the body. If so, report them. Say out loud, "I have a pain in my shoulder." Or, "My foot burns." All of that helps, because it may have a very important connection with Mrs. Jones. You can't know. You may stop and say to yourself, "Oh, this is just my own imagination." But if there's a definite pain there, say so, even if it is your own imagination. There may not be any apparent connection between that pain and Mrs. Jones, and yet, saying that you feel the pain, may in some way relieve some tension in Mrs. Jones. It may just suggest to her that someone is in this with her, but it may have a deeper bearing, too.

Again, if you begin to see pictures or symbols, report them as carefully as you can. "I see this, I see that — I see an ostrich walking", or whatever it may be. And keep your mind quiet — don't get excited about these things - keep your mind quiet and watch and see what happens — it's kind of a quiet procedure, if you're seeing pictures. It's like fishing. And those who are very good at seeing pictures report that it isn't that some new-kind of vision comes to you, but it's that the picture is there in everyone all along, but that most of us have never looked at it. It's right there in front of your eyes. It's the thought picture in your mind that you don't ordinarily look at.

Did you ever suddenly, perhaps while riding on a bus, or sitting down somewhere, realize that in your mind you had been looking at a stained glass window for quite some time? That it's been a background to your thoughts and you just hadn't looked at it until now? Well, that's the way this vision comes. You don't expect it. So, pictures may be your contribution to the group.

Or, your contribution may be that suddenly you feel there's some phrase that has some effect on the individual.

You might speak up and say, "I get the words, 'Get out of here, get out of here,'" and this may have some bearing, it may change the subconscious makeup of Mrs. Jones. Maybe the group leader will decide to have Mrs. Jones repeat that phrase. You may see some scenery that has to do with Mrs. Jones' early life. You may get a picture, just as if her 'E' were showing you a movie of something in her early life. Report it all.

Now, mind you, you don't know whether these things are true, or have any sense to them or not. You're just reporting what you get. And in reporting what you get, you'd be surprised how many Mrs. Joneses get rid of their headaches. And not a one of you has to believe in anything extraordinary about this at all, except that something seems to produce benefit out of just such group activity.

Suppose that you've been having Group-E meetings for quite some time. When you have these meetings for a while, you'll discover that people seem to have natural talents in this field. That is, the person who doesn't know anything about E-Therapy who comes along with somebody else and who is rather skeptical, but who has been dragged into it, lo and behold, that person may begin reporting that he feels pains in the shoulder, a pain here, a pain there, or he may report he sees pictures, or he may be the life of the party before the evening is over. These abilities are natural in some of us, and in some others they are inhibited, but the group sessions themselves may open them up. If you've been having these Group-E meetings for quite some time, then you may discover that people tend to specialize to some degree. That is, you may find that there are some people who seem to get the aches and pains quite a lot. There are others who seem to get the answers to questions or get pictures, and so forth, and answer questions. There are others who seem to get the fire energy or just sit quietly as if they were asleep. If you like, you may divide them into four groups, and then you can do what is called 'Hyper-E' as a team. This is a more specialized thing. It's only possible if you have some people who get answers to questions, who get pictures, or who get phrases. It takes a few of those.

The Group-E that I have mentioned is possible whether you have this or not. But this teamed Hyper-E work is something that is only easy to do if you have some people who can get answers to questions and can get definite pictures. You might divide the people into four groups. If you are the leader of the group, you're the one who's going to ask the questions, so you're the questioner. If there are a couple of people who seem to be good ones to form questions, you can have them sit with you and whisper their questions to you. At first, let the leader ask the questions.

Directly across from the leader should be the people who answer the questions, and there are those who see pictures and get phrases. Put them all in one group. And then, over to the left side, say, put all the people who get pains, breathe heavily, etc. This includes the people who get a tendency to move this way and that way, people who are able to have tensions released through them. On the right, have seated the people that feel fire now and then or who just sit quietly.

We even have some nicknames for these groups. You might say that the fellow that asks the questions is the 'prosecutor', if you like. He 'prosecutes' the case. The people across from him are the 'FBI', they're the ones who give the information. The ones over to the left side of the speaker are those we call the 'grunt and groan' section, the ones that get all the pains, etc. And those over on the right side are known as the 'zombie' department, because so many of them sit there, perfectly quiet. Some report they feel 'fire', etc. In fact, any of the people who report they feel no response of any kind go into the 'zombie' department. They may discover after a few sessions that they are promoted out of it into some other department, but that doesn't mean that the 'zombie' department isn't important. The 'fire'-feeling personnel, being energy-givers, are classed with the 'zombies', but are sometimes called the 'fire' department.

The group is now divided up into these four groups: The leader, who is asking the questions — the 'prosecutor' — or, you can call him the 'examiner', if you like. Across from him the 'FBI' section, the eyes and ears section, so to speak, and then over to the left of him the 'grunt and groan' department; across from them, the 'zombie' detachment. In the middle, on a cot, is the subject — the person who is going to get the 'Hyper-E' treatment. This is a more specialized treatment than you'd get in an ordinary Group-E session, and it does wonders for some people.

Suppose that Mrs. Smith decides that she wants to have a 'Hyper-E' session. She will lie down on the couch, near the prosecutor. The leader, by the way, may not be the person who is asking the questions. He might be in the 'FBI' section or one of the other sections. But the point is, Mrs. Smith's cot is situated right in front of the questioner. The questioner may reach down and place a blanket over her so she will be quite comfortable. Everyone becomes reasonably quiet. And then the questioner addresses the answerers, "Is

75

Mrs. Smith in touch with her E?" They answer in the negative — that is, they usually do. And then the questioner will say, "What prevents?" Or, "What is obstructing?", or a similar question. The answer may come back, "Fear."

Bearing in mind that the 'E's may not want to go into detail as to what the fear is - and leaving it up to the 'E's is an important job for the asker of questions - the questioner then says, "Can this fear be removed, or discharged, or released," and the 'FBI' department may reply, "Yes." The questioner sits back and soon the 'grunt and groan' division may start wheezing and sighing and report a pain here and a pain there, and so forth. Somebody in the 'zombie' detachment may report they're feeling fire from head to toe, or something like that. Then after a while, the questioner will say, "Is it releasing?" The answerers might say, "It's building up," or, "Yes, it's releasing", and after awhile the asker will say, "Is it released yet?", to which the answerers may reply, "Yes," or "Not quite yet."

The questioner may say later, "Is she in touch with her E now?" Answer, "No." "What prevents?" The answer may be a phrase, 'I hate you.' The questioner then leans forward and speaks to the subject, or 'transient', "Mrs. Smith, would you repeat 'I hate you'?" and she obliges by repeating, "I hate you, I hate you, I hate you." It doesn't mean anything to her. She doesn't particularly remember having said it. But immediately the 'grunt and groan' section goes into wheezing and sighing, moaning, and so forth. And maybe somebody over in the 'fire' department reports feeling some 'fire'. Maybe somebody in the answering section will speak up and give another phrase. She will be instructed to repeat that. The questioner may ask, "Is that releasing?" The answer department says, "Yes." The questioner says, "Is she in touch with her E?" "No." "What prevents?" Perhaps another phrase will be stated. The session may go on and on in just this manner, like a team working, and amazing results can be accomplished.

Now, remember this: Suppose the asker says, "Is she in touch with her E?" "No." "What prevents?" "I see a large five pointed star," may be given as the answer. Then the asker has to say, "Does this star represent a problem?" "Yes." "Can the 'E's present solve this problem?" Remember, <u>you don't ask what it is</u>. Maybe the 'E's want to keep it a secret. But you ask, "Can the 'E's take care of it? Can the tension on this problem be released?" "Yes." whereupon the 'grunt and groan' section starts into operation, as does the 'fire' section, while the vision department reports that the star is changing now; it's getting smaller, weaker, or something like that, or that it's gone or is so weak that it's insignificant.

Remember that <u>the person who is asking the questions must never try to probe into the actual nature of the case</u>. That is the business of the 'E's alone — not of the people present. It may be something that the individual would not like to have talked about at all. Now, believe it or not, this Group-E which I have discussed earlier, is the easiest form of therapy for people to do, because total strangers to the whole subject may come into the group and be star performers before the evening is over. Again, the thing which grows out of it, this teamed 'Hyper-E' work, is one of the most powerful instruments of therapy now available to the human race. It can literally do wonders. Cases that are extremely difficult, that cannot be opened in practically any other way, can be opened up by the teamed 'Hyper-E' work.

So, if you have a congenial group, you start out with the Group-E as herein described, and keep on going until you build up to a Hyper-E team. You'll find that you can get wonderful results in helping one another.

I may mention that Mrs. Smith lying there on the cot will be worked on in various ways by the team until by and by the asker will say, "Is she in touch with her E?" And the answer will come, "Yes." "Is that all that's needed for her now?" "Yes." Then he will say, "That's all, Mrs. Smith. You can get up now. Is there anyone else who wants a session?" Mrs. Smith's session may have been ten minutes long, twenty minutes long, or thirty minutes long. The 'E's in charge govern that. But as you see, it's a more specialized sort of thing than the general Group-E itself. Nevertheless, the Hyper-E teamwork cannot very well be done until you have a good answering section, an answering section that can give you clues, and answer 'Yes' or 'No' when such and such a thing is done. But whether you have that or not, you can still engage in the Group-E activity, and the Group-E activity in time may help one or more members of the group to become gifted in such manner as to enable you to do the Hyper-E teamwork. Of course, some of the people who enter into a Group-E session or who come and witness a teamed Hyper-E session (total strangers can get in on that, too; that's perfectly all right) will naturally want to know what E-Therapy is all about. Point out that it's good for them to have private sessions, if they can get somebody they can work with; let them have the little E-Therapy book, if possible, because the more they know about this, the easier it is to take part in the group.

As those of you who have read the E-Book know, you're not expected to <u>believe</u> anything. We're not saying, in the E-Book, what 'E' is. We don't know what 'E' is. It's the 'upstairs' mind. What's upstairs? We don't know. But for those of you who are interested in entertaining group activity in your home or elsewhere — it can even be done in an auditorium with a large number of people - try this Group-E activity, and if you get to the point where you have the right people who can act as question-answerers, and so forth, and are reasonably accurate, those that see visions, get questions, etc., then you can do the teamed Hyper-E, in which people are divided into sections. These sessions are very funny The 'grunt and groan' section gets laughed at all the time; so do some of the others; some of the visions are funny and some of the people laugh. It isn't necessary to have an attitude of seriousness about it. You just keep at the work and have fun while you're doing it. And the fact that someone's life may be saved in the process is fine, that's your main business, but there's no reason why you can't have a good time while you do it.

Suppose, for example, that Mrs. O'Brien comes to your meeting and she says, "My husband is very, very sick in the hospital. He can't come to the meeting. Is there any way you could do anything to help him?" Take a chance on it! After all, you don't know what the limits of the help are. Ask Mrs. O'Brien to lie down on the cot and just keep her mind on her husband. If she's worried about him, it won't be difficult. And then let her act as proxy, or substitute, so to speak, and you can ask the 'E's present to help Mr. O'Brien, using the same words you use in the Group-E: "Let's ask our 'E's to help Mr. O'Brien by sending some energy through us to him, if that will help; or by discharging his tensions through us to the extent that that can be done safely; or by giving us information that may help" — you can do that; or you can just pretend that Mrs. O'Brien is Mr. O'Brien, and you can proceed to act as if Mr. O'Brien were there — at least he's connected with her in thought — we can assume that. You can say, "Is he in touch with his E?" "No." "What prevents?" "An incident." "What is the incident?" It might be someone falling out of a tree, a boy fourteen years old. And then you go on. "Can the tension be taken out of this incident?" "Yes." Then the 'grunt and groan' section sighs, weeps, etc. We've had cases like that, by the way, in which Mr. O'Brien in the hospital was apparently helped. There's no reason why your group shouldn't try it, just to see. If someone comes in and says, "My cousin is sick in a North Korean prison camp. Can we do something to help him?" Before you start out on the case, have the cousin lie down and be proxy, or substitute.

There are all kinds of things you can do. But remember that the main interest of the 'E's is to <u>integrate</u> people. And don't be concerned with doing psychic or telepathic stunts, or anything of that sort. All those things are incidental to the main purpose. We're grown up now. We're not interested in stunts. We're interested in helping one another. That's the main purpose of the whole thing. Don't be concerned with spirit communication. If there are people who are psychics or spiritualists, point out to them that what we call 'E' is the 'Father within', and that all the spirits and all the spirit guides are very much interested in what the Father will do, and they should all be quiet and see what the 'E's do.

You'll find that psychic people and people who have spirit guides in control are very much interested in E-Therapy. It benefits all of them. Then there's the fellow that says, "Well, they don't really have spirit guides in control; it's just part of their own mind." So what? Maybe it is and maybe it isn't. The main thing we're here for is to get <u>integrated</u> and there's no point to indulging in these pet theories as to whether or not such and such a thing is so. In any event, a Group-E activity is not concerned with spirit communication or anything of that sort. It is concerned with helping people. It appears that the 'E's have the power to help people whether they are nearby or far away But investigate that for yourself. Don't take my word for it. Just try it out.

I'd like to give some more general information as to this sort of work, how long it has been going on, how many people do it, and so forth.

Hyper-E was first found out about in August of 1951 and people have done truly wonderful things with it. Group-E appeared, I believe, a little later than that. It was largely developed by Mr. Junius Adams of San Francisco. The Hyper-E was first developed at Fair Oaks, which is situated near Sacramento, California, by Mr. E. G. Robles, Sr. and Mr. E. G. Robles, Jr. and Mr. Ray Goodloe and a few others that they worked with. I learned about Group-E and about Hyper-E from these people, and since that time I have begun to teach it. The most thoroughly trained group, as far as large scale activity is concerned, is one in Portland, Oregon, which can do both Group-E and Hyper-E as a team very well and has been doing quite remarkable things. There is a group of people in San Francisco who can do it, the group at Fair Oaks is still operating, and one in Los Angeles as well. I can't think, off hand, of any other centers that are active in that respect, but this tape is being made so that people all over the country can do it. It's really one of the easiest ways of having an interesting evening at home or in a group and doing something useful at the same time. You don't have to figure out how it's done yourself. Change the slogan, "Let George do it," to "Let E do it." There have even been people released from the insane asylum by having their tensions released through the 'grunt and groan' section. Then, of course, therapy was continued for them after they got out. You might try that, if you like. There are a whole lot of people in asylums that can be helped by having Hyper-E—teamed Hyper-E or Group-E—done for them. Try it and see.

But remember this limitation: The 'grunt and groan' section are people doing what we call 'proxy', of course — that is, they are feeling someone else's pains for them, being a proxy or a substitute. And we have found, at least this seems to be the general rule in regard to it, that if you do proxy for someone, you relieve that person's tensions, but you do <u>not</u> remove the cause of them. So you may take all of the steam out of their tensions and their troubles for a moment. But you must help them with a regular session some time later. So, if you have some friend who, due to some psychic breakdown or other, is in a nearby asylum, mental home or hospital, you can get them out, all right, by relieving their tensions, but after you get them out, be sure they come and have a regular session of some kind so that the cause of their tensions can be released. In other words, we cannot set other people completely free, but only temporarily, through 'proxy.'

Another thing: You notice that I mentioned that we should ask the 'E's to relieve other people's tensions through us to the extent that it can be done safely. It's very important to say 'to the extent that it can be done safely' for this reason: Suppose that there's somebody that you want to do proxy for. If you're in the 'grunt and groan' section, (by the way, you know you can do this 'proxy' privately by yourself for an individual) that is, if you're a person that can pick up tensions from other people and let them out through you, and you have a friend named Fred, who has sinus headaches, and you decide that you want to let Fred's sinus headache tensions out through you — you can do it. Fred may get rid of his sinus headaches quite quickly. And you can do it with ease, provided that you yourself don't have a tendency toward sinus headaches. If you have a tendency toward sinus headaches, then you're going to have a double load, and you'll be sorry.

The reason is this: Fred has sinus headaches because that's a particular kind of tension that he can't get rid of, can't release it, so it piles up in him and gives him sinus headaches. If you don't have sinus headaches, that means that you don't store up that kind of tension; therefore you can act as a drainpipe for Fred and get rid of his sinus headache tensions and it won't disturb you at all. You may feel a little tendency toward a sinus headache temporarily but it's coming through you, not hurting you. But if you have a tendency toward sinus headaches, that means you have the same weakness that Fred has, and if you take on his load, you'll just have a double load. So, always when you want to do 'proxy' for someone, ask his 'E' and your 'E' to let his tensions out through you to the extent that that can be done safely. And the group leader should say that at every time he suggests that tensions be released. He should always say, "Let's ask the 'E's to release Mrs. Jones' tensions through us, to the extent that that can be done safely." You will find that well worthwhile, because these 'E's will permit us to make a mistake. They don't interfere with our freedom at all.

I've been present at quite a number of Hyper-E sessions and Group-E sessions and I'd like to tell you two things that I've learned about 'E's and about the way they work. One is that after you've been in this for quite a while, you begin to realize that these 'E's really are something. Just take your time about it. You may not know when you get through what they are, but you'll know that they're very, very intelligent. There seems to be an incredible mind there in an 'E'.

You'll find that so far as directing the therapy is concerned, that they're very imperious, that they know what they are doing, and if you get out of line in any way, they will tell you off! They are very impersonal, very precise, and it's like being told off by some great surgeon or somebody that knows forty-eight thousand times as much about his trade as you do. They are very imperious that way. But they also have one quality that ordinarily doesn't go with imperious people. That is this: They are very, very scrupulous in protecting your own personal right to privacy. I've mentioned how, that if there is something that you wouldn't want brought out in front of the group, that they bring it out symbolically. I've mentioned that if you want to make a mistake and neglect to ask 'E' to protect you from somebody else's tensions that might bother you, then 'E' will give you the tensions you asked for and they <u>can</u> bother you. That's up to you. They do not interfere with your way of life.

Some people have the feeling, "Oh, I wouldn't want to be dominated by my 'E.'" Well, that's just what you <u>won't</u> be. Your 'E' will not control you. Your 'E' will <u>not</u> take responsibility for you. Your 'E' will help you to become <u>integrated</u>, but your decisions are your own. So, those two things that I have learned, that 'E's are incredibly intelligent creatures (they seem like separate creatures to us), incredibly intelligent and incredibly imperious, but at the same time far more concerned with protecting an individual's personal rights and privacy than the average one of us. So you find those two things.

E's are very tactful. They do not appear to make mistakes, either, by the way. Of all the Group-E sessions that I have seen, the teamed Hyper-E sessions that I have seen, I have never known anyone to be harmed by that kind of activity. Incidentally, there is one limitation to that, and that is that there are some people who seem to pick up other people's pains and troubles too readily, and have difficulty in getting rid of them. Those people you might say have thin skins, somehow. They seem to get these tensions too readily. They aren't necessarily the ones who are getting the therapy. They may be among those who are giving it. You may find some such people. If so, if somebody in your group reports, "Tonight, when I took Mrs. Jones' headache away in the 'grunt and groan' section, it stayed with me," that may be because the group leader has not specifically said that these tensions should be taken only insofar as they could be, handled safely. Or it may be that this individual has a tendency to take too much of people's pains. If so, plunk them down right there and give them a session. Or just call 'E's to their aid in a Group-E session and ask that the 'E's help this person be protected from taking too much tension from other people, or from retaining the tensions of other people. Make a special request for it.

Now suppose somebody comes with a <u>specific</u> problem. We can't really give specific problems to 'E's in the way you might think, because that would be telling them what to do. But there is a way. Suppose that someone wants to make better grades in school. Suppose that you have a high school boy present who wants to make better grades in school. The leader can say, in Group-E, "Let's ask our 'E's to take up the question of Johnny's grades, and do whatever is necessary to help him get better grades in school, if that is the wise thing to do at this time." Always put in a clause like that. That leaves it up to 'E'. "If that is the wise thing to do at this time." Then the 'E's can go ahead.

Or, if you are using teamed Hyper-E, instead of asking the usual question, "Is he in touch with his E?", ask if the 'E's have a recommendation to make, or will they take up the problem of Johnny's grades. Or you can just give him a regular Hyper-E session, saying that Johnny has this particular problem in his mind, and let's go ahead and give him a session, and if that can be handled in this order at this time, why, that is fine and will be appreciated. In other words, <u>don't make the mistake of trying to tell 'E's what to do. They know what to do far better than we do. If you can keep that in mind — that you are not to direct the therapy</u>

—that you are simply to act as the spokesman for the group, then you as a group leader will make no mistakes.

Do not get involved in your own theories — your pet theories. If you are an occultist, for example, and what appears to be occult phenomena manifest, don't go and tell what you think they are, because these are E-phenomena, and 'E's know more about occult phenomena than you do, so you might as well be quiet.

I remember a story about a man of action who was in the presence of a very wise man. This man of action had done everything he could to solve a certain problem. He'd beaten up this person and beaten up that person, and he'd tried to get the answer. And then the wise man said to him, "You've done your best. Now improve on it by allowing me to do mine." That is what 'E's say to us, in effect. Having done our best, we can improve on it by allowing them to do theirs. And in a Group-E or Hyper-E session, that is where the 'E's are doing their best.

I think I've covered most of the points relative to these two types of sessions. As you can see, one is simply the outcome of the other, where things are a little bit more specialized, more concentrated. But let me say again that Group-E is the easiest kind of therapy to get started in, and that the teamed Hyper-E is probably one of the most powerful methods of therapy known in the world today.

I hope that you will try them, and please let me know of the activities of your particular group. Write to me, let me know about what you are doing. I certainly will be very pleased to hear.

Now, I'd like also to mention something that seems to obstruct the progress in therapy of a great many people.

Did you know that your 'E' keeps accounts on you? There was a fellow in Portland, Oregon, who told his brother-in-law that he had had some psychotherapy from some man, about forty-five hours of it. It hadn't done him any good. The brother-in-law said, "Who'd you get it from?" "Oh, from so-and-so." "How much did it cost you?" "Oh, I didn't pay him anything." "Well, did you exchange services with him in any way?" "Why, no, I don't know enough to give that kind of therapy." The brother-in-law said, "Well, you got what you paid for, didn't you?" He got nothing — he paid for nothing.

In the same way, I know of people who are playing these tapes for others and going into debt doing it, because some of you people are taking a free ride. We don't care if you take a free ride. It doesn't concern us. We do this because we like it. But the point is that if you take a free ride, you will get out of your therapy exactly what you pay for, exactly like that fellow in Portland. If you pay for nothing, that's what you'll get. I mention that as an obstacle to your own progress, not because I'm like a bill collector, suggesting that you pay somebody. I don't get anything out of what is paid to hear these tapes; I don't even make anything out of the tapes. I'm just telling you for your own information that hitch-hikers don't get anywhere in therapy, because your 'E' keeps accounts on you.

This ends the reading of the lesson. I hope you've enjoyed it.

Visit

http://www.kitselman.com

for details on other material by A. L. Kitselman as well as further biographical information. The web site also offers many of Kitselman's original audio lectures.

See overleaf for details on the original book
"E-Therapy"

MWI Publishing
do you have

stories to tell

poems to share

information to impart

then together we will make it happen

www.mwipublishing.com

E-Therapy

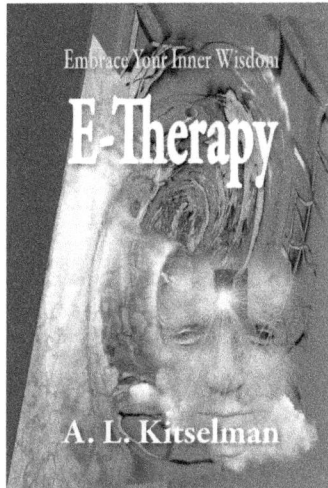

Would you like to ..

Improve your conduct? Is there a habit you'd like to get rid of?

Experience extreme physical pleasure? Intense, ever-fresh happiness? Deep impartial calmness?

Lose the feeling of insecurity? Make an end of doubt and perplexity? Lose all sense of fear, hatred, and grief?

Become a prodigy in science, government, business, art or education? A genius in originality, mental grasp, or in understanding others? Would you like to develop supernormal powers?

Become fully integrated? To be directly aware of things (without needing to sense them or think about them)? To realize a state of being in which there is no obstruction?

These pages tell how.

From Masterworks International Publishing
ISBN: 978-0-9565803-7-5

www.ingramcontent.com/pod-product-compliance
Lightning Source LLC
Chambersburg PA
CBHW030027290326
41934CB00005B/522